EAT LIKE A LOCAL- COLOMBO

Colombo Sri Lanka Food Guide

J. Lorenz

Eat Like a Local-Colonbo Copyright © 2019 by CZYK Publishing LLC. All Rights Reserved.

All rights reserved. No part of this book may be reproduced in any form or by any electronic or mechanical means including information storage and retrieval systems, without permission in writing from the author. The only exception is by a reviewer, who may quote short excerpts in a review.

The statements in this book are of the authors and may not be the views of CZYK Publishing.

Cover designed by: Lisa Rusczyk Ed. D.

CZYK Publishing Since 2011.

Eat Like a Local

Lock Haven, PA
All rights reserved.
ISBN: 9781698273631

Eat Like a Local

BOOK DESCRIPTION

Are you excited about planning your next trip?

Do you want an edible experience? Would you like some culinary guidance from a local? If you answered yes to any of these questions, then this Eat Like a Local book is for you. Eat Like a Local-Colombo by author J. Lorenz gives you the inside scoop on Colombo food. Culinary tourism is an important aspect of any travel experience. Food has the ability to tell you a story of a destination, its landscapes, and culture on a single plate. Most food guides tell you how to eat like a tourist. Although there is nothing wrong with that, as part of the Eat Like a Local series, this book will give you a food guide from someone who has lived at your next culinary destination.

In these pages, you will discover advice on having a unique edible experience. This book will not tell you exact addresses or hours but instead will give you excitement and knowledge of food and drinks from a local that you may not find in other travel food guides.

Eat like a local. Slow down, stay in one place, and get to know the food, people, and culture. By the time you finish this book, you will be eager and prepared to travel to your next culinary destination.

OUR STORY

Traveling has always been a passion of the creator of the Eat Like a Local book series. During Lisa's travels in Malta, instead of tasting what the city offered, she ate at a large fast-food chain. However, she realized that her traveling experience would have been more fulfilling if she had experienced the best of local cuisines. Most would agree that food is one of the most important aspects of a culture. Through her travels, Lisa learned how much locals had to share with tourists, especially about food. Lisa created the Eat Like a Local book series to help connect people with locals which she discovered is a topic that locals are very passionate about sharing. So please join me and: Eat, drink, and explore like a local.

TABLE OF CONTENTS

BOOK DESCRIPTION
OUR STORY
TABLE OF CONTENTS
DEDICATION
ABOUT THE AUTHOR
HOW TO USE THIS BOOK
FROM THE PUBLISHER
1. Arriving In Paradise Isle
2. Money, Money, Money
3. When Walking In Buddha's Land
4. "Alcohol Is The Anesthesia By Which We Endure The Operation Of Life"
5. Do Your Homework
6. Melting Pot
7. Staples
8. Jak & The Breadfruit
9. We Have A Lovely Bunch of Coconuts
10. Banana Leafed Treasures
11. Hitting The Streets
12. Taka-taka-taka-taka....
13. The Dough Way To Being A Local
14. High Tea In The Home Of Ceylon Tea
15. Brunch It Up In Style!
16. Breakfast All Day Long

17. Rush, Rush, Rush… Grab A Quick Lunch
18. Is Every Night 'Date Night' When You Are On Vacation?
19. Bring On The Festivities!
20. Christmas In The Tropics
21. Thai Pongal & Deepavali (Diwali)
22. Id'ul Fitr Festival- Ramadan
23. Did Someone Say 'Biryani'?
24. Finger Food
25. A Taste Of The Far-East In The Not-So Far-East
26. Bento Boxed
27. Green Curry, Red Curry, Yellow Curry…
28. Quando In Italia…
29. Pizza! We Like Pizza!
30. See-food - Sea-food!
31. Keep Crabbing On
32. Prawning Around With Hot Butter Cuttlefish
33. Booze & Bites
34. Bar Hopping
35. A Stickler For The Norm
36. The 'Bean' Of Youth?
37. Themed Cafes
38. A Cup Of Joe And A Good Book Is All One Needs
39. Soul Hungers For Art, Tummy Rumbles For Food…

40. Grub Fest
41. Confessions Of A Chocaholic
42. Is There Even Such A Thing As 'Too Much Sugar'?
43. Love At First Bite
44. Elevate Your Senses
45. Meet For Meat
46. Go Veg
47. After Party Food
48. Good Market, Good Produce, Good Times
49. Getting Fruity
50. Tea-spirations

Bonus Tips

1. Sun, Sand & Surf
2. Kingdom Past
3. Central Highlands
4. Dry Zone
5. Native Lankans in Dambana

Why Visit?

Other Resources:

READ OTHER BOOKS BY CZYK PUBLISHING

DEDICATION

This book is dedicated to my mother who has always been willing to whip up something 'interesting' for me, whenever I get bored with normal Rice and Curry. It is also dedicated to my husband who continually persuades me to step out of my comfort zone and try new things and is always willing to 'cook up a storm' for me.

ABOUT THE AUTHOR

Jenny is a passionate traveller with a flair for the creative. From evoking emotions through music or creating strong sentiments with words, Jenny can take you to a wonderland, which is her very own world.

Jenny loves to travel with her husband who is her globetrotting 'partner in crime'. She is into Yoga and Pilates, but has a love of Chocolate so strong that her body doesn't necessarily reflect the practice of Yoga or Pilates.

Born and raised in Colombo, Sri Lanka she has a busy day job that takes up most of her time. Balancing her new and exciting life as a mom, she still finds the time for freelance writing to keep the creativity flowing and of course to sample the delectable food at new eateries that pop up in Colombo, almost on a weekly basis. While Jenny may not be a typical foodie in the traditional sense, she gets honorary 'foodie' status due to her overwhelming love of 'sugar and spice and everything nice' that only a fellow 'sweet tooth' would be able to relate to.

Whenever time permits, she and her husband along with the new addition to their family, like to travel the world to see and experience different cultures and cuisines, and share the experience with many.

HOW TO USE THIS BOOK

The goal of this book is to help culinary travelers either dream or experience different edible experiences by providing opinions from a local. The author has made suggestions based on their own knowledge. Please do your own research before traveling to the area in case the suggested locations are unavailable.

Travel Advisories: As a first step in planning any trip abroad, check the Travel Advisories for your intended destination.
https://travel.state.gov/content/travel/en/traveladvisories/traveladvisories.html

FROM THE PUBLISHER

Traveling can be one of the most important parts of a person's life. The anticipation and memories that you have are some of the best. As a publisher of the *Eat Like a Local*, Greater Than a Tourist, as well as the popular *50 Things to Know* book series, we strive to help you learn about new places, spark your imagination, and inspire you. Wherever you are and whatever you do I wish you safe, fun, and inspiring travel.

Lisa Rusczyk Ed. D.
CZYK Publishing

Eat Like a Local

"I think food, culture, people and landscape are all absolutely inseparable."

- Anthony Bourdain

Even with nearly three decades of living in Sri Lanka, I'm yet to see and experience everything this beautiful island nation has to offer. This may be the only island in the world that has so many different climatic regions. From the chilly hill country to the dry zone to the wetlands and natural rain forests to the beautiful coastal belt, we truly have got it all.

As there is so very much to see and do within this island nation I may need several books to describe it all in detail, therefore I will be focusing only on Colombo, the business hub of Sri Lanka.

Sri Lanka has a multicultural influence on food based on its very colourful history and a brief outline of the history and races within the island is necessary, to better take you on a culinary journey within the island.

An island kingdom dating back to 5th Century B.C., the Portugese, Dutch and British later colonized Sri Lanka. From the time King Wijaya arrived from India to the land of "Thambapanni" (so called due to the golden sands surrounding the island) to the 16th Century and beyond when the island was under the Europeans, Sri Lanka boasts a rich history and various influences on lifestyle, architecture and most importantly food. Invaded by the Portugese in search of spices, thereafter by the Dutch and finally by the British, Sri Lanka gained independence in 1948, but remained under the British empire until 1972 when it became a republic. In 1978 a constitution was introduced that made the executive president the ruler. In 1983 the riots began based on ethnic conflicts between the majority Sinhala and minority Tamil. The civil war ended in 2009 after nearly 3 decades.

During the Portugese regime (1597-1658), Cinnamon was discovered in Ceylon (now Sri Lanka). The Portugese conquered the reigning Kotte Kingdom and gained control of this precious spice, which is native to Ceylon, until the Dutch overthrew the Portugese and gained control of the Cinnamon trade (1658- 1796). The British took over thereafter and the Cinnamon trade then fell into British hands for the next 2 centuries. By the 1800s Cinnamon had lost its rarity, as Cassia Cinnamon had been cultivated in neighbouring lands. However Ceylon Cinnamon is still the best Cinnamon in the world with its mild flavor and exotic scent. To date 90% of the world's Cinnamon is grown and produced in Sri Lanka.

During the British reign, in 1824 a Tea plant was brought to Ceylon from China and by 1867 the Tea Industry of Ceylon started budding and Ceylon Tea is rated as one of the best Tea in the world.

With this rich history behind us there is no wonder that so many different varieties of food and cuisines have merged and become the "Sri Lankan Food" that we know and love today.

Known for their hospitality, Sri Lankans love to welcome anyone to their island paradise and what better way to do so than, to share our love of food and drink with others?

Things to know:

Former name: Ceylon

Races: Sinhala (majority), Tamil, Burgher (descendants of the Portugese, Dutch and British), Muslim

Religions: Buddhism (main), Hinduism, Christianity, Islam

Languages: Sinhala (main), Tamil, English

Sinhala words to know:
- Hello – Ayubowan (Ah-you-bo-one)
- Thank you- Sthoothi (S-thoo-thi)
- Food- Kaema (Kah- muh)
- Drink- Beema (Bee-muh)

Well known for: Ceylon Tea, Ceylon Cinnamon, Gems

Climate: Humid (average 60%-90% year round)

Eat Like a Local

Temperature:
- Coastal 77 Fahrenheit – 86 Fahrenheit
- Highlands 59 Fahrenheit – 64 Fahrenheit

Monsoon periods:
- South West- May to September
- North East- October to February

Best time to Travel: November to April (season)
Note: Which part of the island you plan to visit should be taken into consideration when booking your travel dates

Currency: Sri Lanka Rupee (LKR)
Note: There are many authorized Foreign Exchange dealers located conveniently at the airport and most towns for the ease of tourists

Dress code: Conservative
Note: Pack light, loose, cotton clothes and sandals / slippers as humidity levels are high

Apps to download:
- Google maps
- 'Uber' & 'Pick Me': to book a cab or 'Tuk Tuk'

How to travel within the city:
- Tuk tuk (book on app or hail along the road)- most convenient
- Cabs (book on app)- relatively cheap and most cab drivers will speak English
- Bus- for a truly local experience (very loud and crowded)
- Train- Fastest mode of transport during rush hour traffic (crowded)

Local Music: Baila (introduced by the Portugese)

Shopping:
- High-end local experience- Barefoot, Paradise Road
- International brands: Selected brands available at most shopping malls
- Souvenirs- Odel (for quirky, modern items), Lakpahana (for more traditional items)

Eat Like a Local

Where to stay:
- Hotels
- Air BnB
- Serviced apartments
- Hostels / bunks

Pictures to take in Colombo:
- The ever developing Colombo skyline
- Independence square
- Colombo port city (currently being built)
- Lotus Tower
- Old Cargills building (heritage site)
- Old post office building (heritage site)

Colombo
Sri Lanka

Eat Like a Local

Colombo Climate

	High	Low
January	88	74
February	89	75
March	89	76
April	89	78
May	89	79
June	87	79
July	86	79
August	86	78
September	86	78
October	87	76
November	87	75
December	87	75

GreaterThanaTourist.com

Temperatures are in Fahrenheit degrees.
Source: NOAA

Eat Like a Local

1. ARRIVING IN PARADISE ISLE

Hovering over the island prior to taxiing down the runway you will catch your first glimpse of this tear drop shaped island, sitting pretty in the middle of shimmering Blue waters, with Coconut trees and Golden sands bathed in cheery sunshine. While you are eagerly waiting to jump right into your adventure in paradise, getting about in a foreign country where English isn't the mother tongue may not be the easiest and may get you down. A few tips on what to do when you arrive will keep you feeling happy and continue that eager anticipation of exploring paradise. Although English isn't the native language, fear not as many locals are fluent in English and others can manage to get out a few broken sentences to at least give you basic instructions / directions when needed.

First and foremost, you need currency. There are Banks within the airport that will assist you with this. Secondly, you need to sort out your transport from the airport to your preferred destination. There are cabs available from the airport, or you can book a cab via 'Uber' or 'Pick Me' (the local version of Uber). The cabs you book via the apps will accept card or cash, however cabs that you book from the airport or hail along the road will not accept card payments. Once you reach the hustle and bustle of Colombo, the easiest mode of transport would be 'Tuk Tuks'. You can book tuk tuks via Uber and Pick Me as well.

Sri Lanka with its multicultural presence has roads named after many important people and most of the time they are long and unreadable. The best way to know if you are on the correct path to your destination would be to track your movement via Google Maps. Just select your destination and the app will show you the route and also show you how to avoid congestion, because traffic tends to build up quite heavily in and around Colombo.

Sri Lankan weather is mainly year round humidity. There are 2 monsoon periods and

Eat Like a Local

the hottest months are March and April. Which part of the island you plan to visit should be carefully planned according to the season and monsoon periods, unless of course the sole purpose of visiting the island is to experience a tropical island monsoon.

Lonely Planet named Sri Lanka as the number 1 destination in 2019 and this stands despite the 2019 terror attacks during Easter celebrations. Many countries have softened travel warnings against Sri Lanka, but always check travel warnings when booking flights. Sri Lanka had its share of suffering and difficult periods, but it stands strong and has rebuilt itself over the past ten years since the end of the civil war and is well worth a visit.

2. MONEY, MONEY, MONEY

All major foreign currencies can be easily converted within the island. It is recommended to use authorized dealers for this purpose and there is no shortage of them in and around Colombo When paying by cash, only Sri Lankan Rupees will be accepted, and almost all places accept card payments. There will be a significant government tax of VAT and NBT along with a service charge totaling to approximately 33%, but it is still accepted that a tip be left for your server. As Sri Lanka is a hospitable nation, all servers, barring a handful, will go out of their way to please you and serve you well. They do not expect a tip when doing this however they will be incredibly grateful with whatever you give them, as they have a hard life. Most have left their villages and families behind and moved to the city in search of an income and every cent is saved to take back to their villages.

3. WHEN WALKING IN BUDDHA'S LAND

Sri Lanka is a Buddhist country and though the law doesn't specifically state it, it would be best if you avoid wearing any clothing with pictures of Lord Buddha. If you have any tattoos of Lord Buddha it is advisable that you wear clothing items to cover them up, as locals may find it offensive when the holy personage they worship at temples is depicted on anyone's clothes or body parts. Overall it is advisable that you try to cover up as much as possible when travelling in Sri Lanka. This does not mean you have to cover up from head to toe as it is incredibly hot and humid in Sri Lanka, especially in Colombo. Strappy tops and shorts are acceptable as long as there isn't too much cleavage or thigh showing. To beat the heat and humidity it is advisable to wear loose, light, breathable fabrics like cotton or linen.

4. "ALCOHOL IS THE ANESTHESIA BY WHICH WE ENDURE THE OPERATION OF LIFE"

Sri Lankans are no exception to that quote by George Bernard Shaw. We are a booze-loving nation and are capable of making some pretty potent drinks. The mildest of them being Beer and the strongest being Moonshine (Kasippu as it is known in Sinhala).

There really is nothing better than an ice cold Lion Beer on a humid day in Sri Lanka, preferably on the beach. Foreign liquor is also available for purchase freely within the island though the tax is much higher. Also if you wish to buy some bottles at Duty Free when you are arriving in the island, make sure to check the quota that is allowed in to the country per passport.

Many places have happy hours and 2 for 1 drinks offers. Make the most of these and try as many international and local spirits as you can. Make sure to have the apps mentioned above downloaded and ready to use when it's time to head back to your lodgings and sleep it off.

Bear in mind that being a Buddhist nation, Full Moon 'Poya' Days are excise holidays and you will not be able to purchase any liquor at restaurants, while bars and liquor shops are closed.

5. DO YOUR HOMEWORK

When planning your trip to any place including Sri Lanka, make sure to research, review and plan ahead. There are many ways to research online about your

Eat Like a Local

travel destination and there is no end of details about Sri Lanka online as well. If in doubt you can always check Lonely Planet and Explore Sri Lanka. For reviews about places to visit and things to do there's always online review sites such as pulse and yamu (which means 'Let's go' in Sinhala) There are also subsectors in this site called "Kamu" (which means 'Let's eat') for restaurant reviews and "Bomu" (which means "Let's drink") for reviews on places you can get your drink on.

6. MELTING POT

In the brief historic outline provided earlier it is apparent that Sri Lanka is truly a multicultural, ethnically vibrant land and all the historic influences have led to a very aromatic and tasteful cuisine that has its roots in near and far reaching lands, from the southern parts of our neighbouring India to Europe. A respect towards all races and religions is expected within the island and it should be borne in mind that eating habits among the various races differ. While most places offer Pork, there are some who will not serve Pork in keeping with Islamic teachings. Beef is generally consumed, but there may be certain Buddhists and Hindus who do not wish to consume Beef. So you may come across a few restaurants where you would find only poultry and seafood on the menu.

7. STAPLES

Our everyday meal and staple diet is Rice, and we have some extensive varieties to share with you! History says that over 400 types of rice were cultivated in Sri Lanka in days gone by. Now, there are only a few strains of hybrid rice varieties from Brown rice which Sri Lankans call Red rice, to White rice. Rice and Curry is the main meal for locals, probably originating from South India, but curries made in Sri Lanka are not the same as Indian curries. For a traditional Sri Lankan meal "Nuga Gama" at Cinnamon Grand is the place to go. I always feel as though I have travelled far out of Colombo to some unheard of village while in fact being very much in the heart of Colombo, as the place is set to resemble a typical Sri Lankan village. Be prepared to taste spicy food and see a lot of Bananas (Sri Lankans go

Eat Like a Local

bananas over Bananas and there's no wonder about it as Sri Lanka proudly lays claim to 29 varieties of Bananas. As all Sri Lankans know, no one can ever escape a hand of Bananas being borne on a tray and presented to them with a cup of Tea when visiting anyone in this country). Bonus Tip: Instead of napkins, Nuga Gama hands out sheets of paper to wipe the hands with after washing the fingers (as locals eat with their fingers), and this doesn't really do anything in the way of absorbing the moisture from the fingers so I always make sure to carry a pack of tissues in my pocket.

For a less expensive meal of traditional rice and curry in a humble setting, there are plenty of places along the roadside where you can get the true "gamey kade" taste (pronounced as Gah-May Kah-Day which means 'Village Shop'). One of my personal favourites is the "Chimney" which is a home run food outlet on Perahera Mawatha, close to the Gangarama temple, so if you wish to see the Gangarama temple and then have a quick and tasty rice and curry meal this is the perfect spot.

8. JAK & THE BREADFRUIT

Along with Rice, Lankan cuisine also boasts of Jak Fruit, which is consumed in various forms. For those who are too impatient to wait for the fruit to mature and prefer to consume it while tender, it's called 'Polos'. Polos curries are available in many of the aforementioned 'Gamey Kade's. For those who wish to sample just the taste of Polos without the heaviness of a rice and curry meal, there are some easy options of Polos sandwiches and Polos wraps. My all time favourite is the Polos Puff which was available at 'The Bakery' at Waters Edge in Battaramulla, however they do not sell it to walk in customers anymore. Now a pre-order is required for a significant number of Polos puffs. So the next best option for a quick 'Polos' fix, would be the Polos sandwich at 'Barista' coffee shop or the Polos wrap at 'The Good Market Saturday Event' at Racecourse Mall.

The mature stage of the Jak Fruit is called 'Kos' and this is a local favourite, from the flesh of the fruit to the seeds of the fruit, prepared in many ways. The over ripe stage of Jak Fruits is called 'Waraka' (promounced 'Wah-Ruh-Kah') and is an acquired

Eat Like a Local

taste. As for me, I run away from it due to its pungent aroma, similar to, but not as intense as Durian.

Whether mythical or factual we will never know, but it is believed that the Dutch introduced Bread Fruit to Ceylon as they found locals to have immense strength by consuming Jak Fruit, and they wanted to diminish the strength of the locals. In the process they ended up giving us yet another yummy dish, which the locals call 'Dhel' (pronounced 'They- l'). Fry up some Dhel chips or cook it in a yummy curry, whatever you decide to do with it, it's simply Yum!

9. WE HAVE A LOVELY BUNCH OF COCONUTS

Sri Lankans love to get coco-nutty! We use it in everything! The milk of the coconut is extracted and used for cooking curry, coconut shavings are used to make coconut sambol (Pol Sambol in Sinhala) We even use copious amounts of Coconut in desserts. In any rice and curry meal you are sure to find freshly grated coconut sambol, which is quite spicy. Slap it in between 2 slices of bread with some cheese and a fried egg and you've got yourself a yummy sandwich. But the best way to taste Pol Sambol is with Roast Paan (pronounced 'Par-n') a 'somewhat' flat bread which is a local favourite. 'Tosakanth's Roast Paan' down De Fonseka Place, Colombo 4 is a must for an out of this world experience.

Sri Lanka is the only country that is home to the king of all Coconuts. King Coconut is a type of Coconut native to Sri Lanka and it has an instant cooling effect in the intense humidity of Colombo. It is sweeter than Coconuts and has an Orange hue to its outer skin. It is known as 'Thambili' in Sinhala, which incidentally is the Sinhala name of the colour 'Orange'. You can find King Coconuts for sale along the roadside and some restaurants serve it as well. It is best in its natural form. For a slightly more elaborate version, 'Diyatha Uyana' near Waters Edge Battaramulla, serves a blended Thambili. It is chilled and blended with ice and some sugar and is refreshingly cold.

Eat Like a Local

10. BANANA LEAFED TREASURES

'Lamprais' is a Dutch creation in Ceylon, using Ceylonese produce and Ceylon spices. Pronounced as 'lump-rye' it is a Dutch word, which loosely translates to 'packet of food'. There are many varieties of Lamprais available in many places in Sri Lanka but the true, authentic Lamprais can be found at the 'Dutch Burgher Union (DBU) Café' at Thunmulla Junction. This aromatic, fist sized, Banana leaf wrapped parcel of delectable food is one of the last remaining links to our Dutch lineage. A personal favourite is the mixed Lamprais. Calling ahead and booking this prior to 11.00 am for lunch that very day is advisable as there is a limited number of parcels that get snatched up quickly.

If you are unfortunate and miss out on getting your hands on a Lamprais, don't get dishcartened because the DBU Café also has an amazing Ghee Rice with 'to die for' Black Pepper Pork. Yum!

11. HITTING THE STREETS

The South Indian influence on Sri Lankan cuisine is apparent when sampling street food. We have the usual Indian street food of Wada and Dosa, along with a local version of the Indian Appam, which in Sri Lanka is called Aappa (pronounced 'Arp-puh') It is called 'Hoppers' in English. Hoppers are made from a rice flour mixture in the shape of a dome. It comes in plain form, with an egg in the center, with grated cheese in the center, with honey in the batter, with Jaggery mixed in… in so many forms and available in every street food outlet around the island. It's normally eaten with 'lunu miris' which is chopped onions and a heart-stopping amount of Red Chili, but it can also be eaten with curry, usually meat or fish.

For a true street food experience, my personal favourite for nearly 3 decades has been from a little family owned joint adjoining the Dehiwela medical center which has the wispiest, crispiest hoppers with the most amazing Kiri-maalu curry (Fish curry that is not spicy). For a more upscale version of street food, visit Kaema-Sutra at the Shangri-La Colombo or

Eat Like a Local

Upali's at Colombo 7. When dining at Kaema-Sutra a worthwhile dessert is the Chocolate hopper, which has a hearty amount of chocolate chips melted in to the center of the Hopper with whipped cream drizzled around it.

12. TAKA-TAKA-TAKA-TAKA....

... a sound that brings joy to any Lankan, anywhere in the world. It's the sound of 'Koththu' being made.

Koththu is a street food that can also be found in any street food outlet around the island and comes in many varieties. It is roti cut up with vegetables, egg and meat and drizzled in spicy gravy. Sometimes, it is also made with String Hoppers instead of Roti or even with Macaroni!

'Kottu Labs' on Nawala Road, Nugegoda (near the open university) is a personal favourite as they offer more than just the basic Koththu varieties seen at street food outlets. Vegetarian options are also available.

13. THE DOUGH WAY TO BEING A LOCAL

Ever heard of Short Eats? probably not, unless you know a Sri Lankan. Short Eats are what locals call snacks. It is most often than not made of bread or puff pastry with some form of meat or vege filling. To truly be christened as a local you will need to sample 'short eats' at some point during your trip. The best 'short eat' of them all, would be the Sri Lankan 'Chinese Roll'. It has absolutely nothing to do with China and if you ask a Chinese person about Chinese Rolls they will be left scratching their heads trying to figure out what you mean. However if you ask a Sri Lankan what a Chinese Roll is they will tell you it is a crumb coated pan roll, deep-fried to a Golden crisp, fondly known as Chinese Rolls by locals. For the best of these 'Chinese Rolls' Hotel Nippon in Slave Island serves up an amazing Mutton roll. I'm salivating just typing about it. For a person who generally doesn't eat Mutton, I can pack away a couple of them in a

Eat Like a Local

heartbeat. If you really are not too fond of consuming Mutton, you can try the Beef roll, which is equally good. However the Mutton roll is iconic.

Hotel Nippon is the one of the first five hotels in Colombo. It was initially built as apartments for the British during their reign over Ceylon, known back then as 'Manning Mansions'. Recently renovated with painstaking attention to detail to preserve the old architecture, the place is worth a visit to see the Burma Teak staircase preserved for over a century and the antique grandfather clock.

14. HIGH TEA IN THE HOME OF CEYLON TEA

The British influence on Sri Lankan culture is apparent when you consider the many places that offer High Tea. Having had the fortune of sampling a Cream Tea in London, England, I can honestly say that Sri Lanka does a bang up job of High Tea as well. In fact, there are certain places that fuse in some local tastes for the Sri Lankan palete.

For a traditional High Tea the best would be at the Galle Face Hotel. Galle Face Hotel started out as Galle Face house which was a villa for the Dutch, so named as it is facing the Galle Face Green (a half kilometer stretch along the West Coast of the island, in the heart of the business capital: Colombo). The hotel was built in 1864 by the British and to this day remains intact, although extensive renovations have been done to maintain the building.

15. BRUNCH IT UP IN STYLE!

Yet another British influence… They say Breakfast is the most important meal of the day. But who can wake up on time for Breakfast when on vacation? Happily, there are some amazing Brunches at many hotels in and around Colombo. The best Brunch I have ever been to would be the Sunday Brunch at the Kingsbury Hotel. Oh! The spread of food! I feel as though I need eyes in the back of my head to see all the food spread around and sadly, I just don't have the capacity to even get through half of the spread. There is something for everyone at this brunch from Oysters to Sushi to a traditional roast

Eat Like a Local

along with everyone's favourite Brunch drink; 'Mimosas'.

16. BREAKFAST... ALL DAY LONG

Just in case your day doesn't start off right unless you sit down at the Breakfast table, but you still want to sleep in… don't worry. Get your beauty sleep and wake up at any time during the day, as there are several places that serve all day breakfast. A dedicated spot would be 'One Up All Day Breakfast' in Colombo 4, or 'Café Kumbuk' in Colombo 7.

17. RUSH, RUSH, RUSH... GRAB A QUICK LUNCH

Rice and Curry is every local's lunch. Majority of the locals bring a 'packet of rice' to work daily, cooked at home and hastily packed before their long commute in to Colombo, in never ending traffic. But for those like myself who sometimes just don't have the time to sit down to eat Rice and Curry, I find

'Brew 1867' at World Trade Center and Nawam Mawatha, an excellent option to grab a quick bite, from Sandwiches to Pasta to Salads. All freshly made that very day and conveniently packed in eco friendly cardboard boxes.

18. IS EVERY NIGHT 'DATE NIGHT' WHEN YOU ARE ON VACATION?

If so, then you are in luck as there is no end of romantic Dinner spots in Colombo. If flickering Candlelight and privacy is what you are looking for The Courtyard- Tintagel in Colombo 7 or The London Grill at Cinnamon Grand are good options for something on the pricier side. For a medium range date night Rare Bar & Restaurant on Park Street or The Gallery Café at Alfred Place, are equally romantic. August by Mama Aida's is an Arabic Food restaurant that romances the soul with its beautiful surrounding and satisfies the tummy with delectable food. Calling ahead and making a reservation is a must as there is limited seating and time slots during which one can dine.

Eat Like a Local

19. BRING ON THE FESTIVITIES!

With Sri Lanka being a cultural melting pot it comes as no surprise that there are many religious festivals and with it, various types of treats! Being a predominantly Sinhala nation the main holiday is the Sinhala and Tamil New Year celebrated in April, known as "Aluth avurudda" (pronounced 'Ah-lu-th Ow-ru-dda') or "Avurudu" (pronounced 'Ow-ru-du)'. There are many tasty treats during this time period and some of my favourites are 'Kavum' (pronounced 'Kah-oom') which is a small oil cake and Kokis, which is a crispy, crunchy delight! Kavum should ideally be eaten while hot. It has a golden, crispy outer layer, while the inside is soft and moist. Kokis comes in savoury and sweet forms. Savoury is the easily found option, while Chocolate Kokis is a lot harder to get your hands on. Try Cinnamon Grand for Chocolate Kokis if ever in Colombo in April.

For year round Avurudu treats, 'Lakpahana' opposite Race Course Mall at Cinnamon Gardens has pre packed treats ready to go. I wouldn't limit myself to just Kavum and Kokis though… I would go nuts and stuff my face with everything from Aasmi, to Kalu Dodol, to Mung Kavum.

20. CHRISTMAS IN THE TROPICS

Many may find it surprising that Christmas is celebrated in Sri Lanka, but the fact is the Portugese introduced Christianity to Ceylon. Sri Lanka boasts some beautiful churches that are fully worth a visit, such as St. Lucia's Cathedral in Colombo 13. Along with Christmas come snugger clothes and leaner wallets because we all splurge on many thing including large quantities of food.

While you get your usual Christmas cookies and Eggnog and Yule log in Sri Lanka there is something unique to Sri Lanka that needs to be tried out during Christmas. The Dutch gifted Ceylon with 'Breudher', which is a steamed cake, made with Currants and Ceylon Cinnamon, eaten warm with drippy butter and slice of Cheddar. Yum! Many Sri Lankans will argue about the best place to get Breudher but the best place has and always will be 'Perera and Sons'. It needs to be steamed before consuming, as it is not sold as a steamed cake.

Sri Lankans also refer to Fruit Cake fermented in Brandy as 'Christmas Cake' and a crowd pleaser called 'Love Cake' which is a delicious confection of Cashew, Pumpkin Preserve and Semolina. My mom bakes the most amazing Love Cake, which I think is all the more tasty as it includes the key ingredient of 'love'. Christmas cake and Love cake are available at almost every bakery in Colombo during the season and there are many home bakers who jump on the bandwagon too. It is easy to find them on Facebook and place an order online.

21. THAI PONGAL & DEEPAVALI (DIWALI)

With a minority Tamil population in Sri Lanka the festivities are on during Thai Pongal and Diwali, which Sri Lankans refer to as 'Deepavali'. During the Thai Pongal celebrations the main celebratory food is a sweet rice pudding known as 'Pongal'. It is not easy to get your hands on this tasty dish and it's prepared by home bakers, most often.

During Deepavali (the festival of lights) there are many traditional Indian sweets that are served but my favourite is 'Gulab Jamun'. The best Gulab Jamun I have tasted, was made by a friend's mom, but as I do not like to trouble her whenever I get a craving for this guilty pleasure, the best option is to buy Gulab Jamun from 'Bombay Sweet Mahal' in Wellawatte.

Bonus Tip: They also serve up a piping hot Beef Samosa that always leaves me hankering for more.

22. ID'UL FITR FESTIVAL- RAMADAN

Sri Lankan Muslims celebrate Ramadan in Sri Lanka and every Sri Lankan looks forward with great anticipation to get 'Watalappam' (pronounced 'What-a-lup-pum') dish from their Muslim friends. It is a Sri Lankan custard pudding made with coconut milk, spices and Jaggery.

It originated with Sri Lankan Malays who came to the island during the Dutch era. It is not always easy to get a really good Watalappam but a home baker does justice to this humble custard pudding and can be found via their website, simply named after the dessert itself. Watalappan.lk

23. DID SOMEONE SAY 'BIRYANI'?

If there is one thing Sri Lankans love more than Rice and Curry it has got to be Biryani. True, it is not a native dish, and it's origins lie in India. History says that the Muslims from South India brought this super tasty dish to Sri Lanka. Weirdly though, majority of Sri Lankans will insist on calling it 'Buriyani' (pronounced 'Boo-ri-yani'). Try 'Pot Biryani' in Dehiwela and Pelawatte for an easy pick up or delivery option (you also get to keep the Clay pot the Biryani is served in) or 'Hotel de Buhari' in Maradana for a Biryani recipe enjoyed by generation after generation of Sri Lankans as it is one of the oldest spots in Colombo who serve a tasty Biryani.

Bonus Tip: Almost all places that serve Biryani will serve Watalappam for dessert.

We also have a bit of middle-eastern flavours working their way through Sri Lanka. 'Arabian Knights' is a favourite for a quick meal while 'August by Mama Aida' is for a more romantic setting as mentioned above.

24. FINGER FOOD

When in South Asia, eat as the South Asians do. We use our fingers when eating Rice and Curry. There is an art to eating with one's fingers. Only the tips of the fingers are used (ideally no food should go beyond the first link (distal phalanx) of the fingers), only one hand is used (the Right hand unless you are Left handed) and we do not believe in licking our fingers clean after a meal.

If you dine out and decide to eat with your fingers, you can request for a 'finger bowl' to wash up after you are done. This will be a decorative bowl with warm water and slice of lime to get rid of the curry scent from your fingers. Some restaurants may have sinks in place to wash your hands after a meal.

Eat Like a Local

If you are truly uncomfortable with eating with your fingers you can always request for cutlery. Every restaurant in Sri Lanka that caters to the Rice and Curry cravings of the local, will provide you with a Spoon and Fork, so you can rest assured.

25. A TASTE OF THE FAR-EAST IN THE NOT-SO FAR-EAST

Who doesn't love Asian food? Sri Lanka boasts a plethora of various Asian cuisines. But it appears that everyone's favourite is Chinese food. And just like the 'Chinese Roll' mentioned earlier, we have our own version of Chinese food. Many street food outlets will throw together some steamed Basmati rice with some Sweet and Sour Meat and Chili Paste and call it Chinese food.

But for the real deal, '88' in Havelock Town or 'Moon River' in Thimbirigasyaya are among the best. Most hotels in Colombo have Dim Sum, for the best options try 'Shang Palace' at the Shangri La Colombo or 'Long Feng' at Cinnamon Lakeside.

26. BENTO BOXED

Who doesn't love Japanese food? Even if you can't stomach raw fish they serve plenty of cooked food that is easier to swallow down.

A local favourite is the Bento Box and there are so many places that offer Bento boxes for those who are caught in a 9-5 rat race. Unlike in Australia, UK and the likes, Sushi hasn't still found its way on to shelves in food outlets in a 'grab & go' fashion. Instead, those who crave some Japanese food need to specifically visit the places that serve Japanese food or get it delivered via Uber Eats or Pick Me Food.

Some of my favourite places for Japanese food are 'Iko-Tei' at the Dutch Hospital Shopping Precinct for an out of this world California Maki and 'Kami Maki' in Colombo 7 where they serve up Japanese Fusion Food. A personal favourite is the Crunchy Salmon Roll at Kami Maki.

Eat Like a Local

27. GREEN CURRY, RED CURRY, YELLOW CURRY...

Thai, Thai, Thai! No introductions necessary for Thai food. My personal favourite is Green Curry while loads prefer the spicier Red Curry. Whatever your preference is, have we got some amazing Thai food right, here in Colombo! 'Boulevard' on Queen's Road is the best place in my humble opinion. Bonus Tip: The Ambarella juice served at Boulevard is delicious! Royal Thai at Cinnamon Lakeside can also claim bragging rights for the best Thai in Colombo.

If Thai isn't quite the thing for you we have a few other Asian cuisines. If what you crave for is Vietnamese we have 'Pho' in Colombo 5, or do you prefer Korean? There's 'Han Gook Gwan' or 'Kang's Kitchen' also in Colombo 5. Indian? 'Mango Tree' at Colombo 7 or for a humble, low cost meal my absolute favourite is 'Elite' in Colombo 3 and 4 for the best Garlic Naan or 'Shanmugas' at the Crescat Boulevard Food Court (Vegetarian food). Try the Paper Dosa, which is served with Sambal. The food is served on a large Silver tray, and it is crowded and loud in the food court and eating is messy as you need to eat with your fingers, but your taste buds will thank you at the end of it all.

28. QUANDO IN ITALIA...

   Well, luckily we Sri Lankans don't have to go to Italy to savour a few yummy Italian recipes. Whether you are a kid or someone with a more refined palete, everyone loves Pizza, Pasta, Lasagna and the likes. 'Dolce Italia' in Colombo 5 is a personal favourite. The best dishes would be the Spinach and Ricotta Ravioli and the Creamy, Shrimp Fettuccine. The chef makes the Pasta fresh and throws in a bit of amore to make an exceptional taste sensation.

   A favourite date-night option for my husband and I is 'Bayleaf' down Gregory's Road, Colombo 7. 'Rocco's' in Nawala does a fair job of Italian dishes too. For pricier options with greater ambience, 'Echo' at Cinnamon Grand and 'Il Ponte' at Hilton Colombo are the places to go.

Eat Like a Local

29. PIZZA! WE LIKE PIZZA!

Echoing Joey Tribbiani right there. Is there any such thing as the perfect Pizza? I believe there is! And it is right here in Colombo. In all seriousness, 'Giovanni's' pizza is incredible! It's a tiny roadside Pizza joint in Thimbirigasyaya with a wood fired oven and chef with a passion. The menu is written in chalk on Blackboards on either side of the entrance. There is limited seating space and it is not surprising to see people along the pavement or leaning up against their cars, devouring Giovanni's pizza. I can eat an entire Pizza myself and sometimes 'pull a Joey' and order a Joey Special (2 pizzas) in one sitting.

Harpo's Black Box Pizza is another go-to if you would like your Pizza delivered to your doorstep.

30. SEE-FOOD – SEA-FOOD!

When you visit an island what do you expect other than amazing Seafood? For a unique sight, head to the coast, to see Sri Lankan stilt fishermen. There's nothing quite like eating a fresh Fish dish on the beach, where you can smell the sea and have your meal, with the salty sea breeze blowing through your hair. 'Sea food cove' at Mount Lavinia Hotel is excellent for this and it is recommended to go for Dinner as it will be cooler than during a blistering hot afternoon.

'Sea Spray' at Galle Face Hotel is another favourite where I actually feel the salty spray from the sea washing over me, while I eat. For a less pricier option 'Wadiya' at Colombo 6 draws a large number of people even with its humble setting of wooden benches and rustic tables, simply due to the amazing sea-food cooked up then and there.

Eat Like a Local

31. KEEP CRABBING ON

Sri Lanka is the home of the Singapore Chili Crab. That's right! Those Golden claws are imported from Sri Lanka. The Sri Lankan style of cooking crab is quite different from Singapore style Chili crab. We are the authority on Crabs in the South Asian region, we even have a ministry for it. Ha ha! 'Ministry of Crab' at the Dutch Hospital Shopping Precinct ranks at number 35 on the 'Top 50 restaurants in Asia' list for 2019. Advance booking is necessary as the tables are always reserved and there are very few walk in customers who are lucky enough to get a table. For the best Crab experience, Ministry of Crab takes pre orders to ensure that the large crabs are saved and prepared for those who order in advance. Latecomers will be served the smaller sized crabs.

When unable to get a table at Ministry of Crab, instead of getting crabby about it, I just go to 'Fat Crab' down Marine Drive for an equally tasty, less crowded option.

32. PRAWNING AROUND WITH HOT BUTTER CUTTLEFISH

No visit to Sri Lanka is complete without trying our Hot Butter Cuttlefish (HBC). A bar favourite, the best place to get this would be at 3 separate restaurants right on the beach! 'Wadiya', 'The Station' and 'Barracuda'. It pairs well with a chilled Lion Beer. HBC is Calamari, batter fried to a Golden crunchiness and is a lip smacking, mouth watering feast! It is generally served on a bed of Onion and Onion leaves and is divine!

We also have succulent prawns in abundance. 'Isso' at Colombo 3 is a 'prawn-tastic' experience where you are able to choose which style you would like your prawns to be cooked. You even get to pick the size of your prawns. Add a carb such as rice or bread, and choose a meal option. A personal favourite is the 'Sweet Potato Fries' to perfectly complement the 'isso' (Sinhala word for Prawns).

Eat Like a Local

33. BOOZE & BITES

The Sri Lankan 'Bite'. No it does not mean we Lankans go around biting people, it is simply food that perfectly complements ones chosen beverage. The aforementioned HBC is one of these 'bites'. There is even a Hot Butter Mushroom for the Vegetarian boozers.

Bites range from salted Peanuts to Murukku (which is a savoury, crunchy snack that originated in India and is very popular in Sri Lanka) to other items which require more preparation such as Chicken wings, devilled Sausages, Omelette and Cutlets (a deep fried croquette) to name a few.

Sri Lanka produces a lot of alcoholic beverages but a special mention has to be made about Lion Beer, which any Sri Lankan would agree is the best brew, Arrack and Coconut Toddy. There are a few bars in Colombo that offer the typical Sri Lankan 'booze and bites' experience. 'Taphouse by R&R' at the Dutch Hospital Shopping Precinct & 'Floor by O!' at CH&FC offer up some local 'bite' options.

34. BAR HOPPING

For an upscale booze and tapas experience in Colombo, head over to 'Curve Bar' at Park Street Mews, 'In..On the Green' at Galle Face Hotel is also great for some live music.

Bar menus in Colombo offer pretty much the usual Sandwiches and Burgers etc. If you have been to one you have pretty much been to all. The defining fact is the live music and prices, which draw in a certain crowd.

'Botanik Rooftop Bistro & Bar' at Hospital Street, Colombo 1 is a bit more on the pricier side, thereby curtailing the crowd to those who are well off.

Bonus Tip- 'Park Street Mews' boasts many restaurants with various cuisines, from Italian, to Japanese to fusion food and a few bars.

35. A STICKLER FOR THE NORM

When in doubt, stick with the familiar. Mc Donald's, Burger King, KFC, Pizza Hut, Dominos, BreadTalk, Coffee Bean & Tea Leaf, Delifrance and TGI Fridays are the more popular franchises in Sri Lanka

But for those of you who are willing to try something different, there are some pretty amazing chefs in this part of the world who can turn out some amazing dishes to tantalize your taste buds. For instance if what you want more than anything else is to sink your teeth into a big, juicy burger then a gourmet burger from my favourite place, Whight & Co. on Marine drive is just right. This is a family friendly place where anyone can bring along a board game and spend some time with loved ones over a friendly game of Monopoly, while sampling some yummy dishes.

36. THE 'BEAN' OF YOUTH?

Having a cup of Coffee is as good as finding the fountain of youth! Or so scientists believe. It is supposed to slow down ageing and prevent weight gain! Whether you accept this or not, who doesn't love a hot cup of Java?

Colombo boasts a number of Coffee shops, just like any other country. We may not have the usual Starbucks, Tim Hortons or Gloria Jeans (though Gloria Jeans did try and fail to get a foot in through the door), but we do have some home grown Coffee Shops that are pretty awesome. 'The Commons Coffee House' on Flower Road is a favourite among many, not just for the Coffee but for the wide variety of food as well. 'The Embazzy' is fairly new and is also located on Flower Road and the Coffee is great. It is freshly ground, 'on ground', and the aroma is heavenly!

Some history for you history buffs, Coffee was actually grown in Sri Lanka before Tea. In 1860 Sri Lanka (then Ceylon), Brazil and Indonesia were the three largest Coffee producers in the world. But the

Eat Like a Local

devastating 'Coffee Leaf Rust' fungal disease that ruined crops in Asia didn't spare Sri Lankan crops either. Coffee was soon replaced by Tea and as of now Sri Lanka has dropped to the 48th largest producer of Coffee in the world. However, Coffee production is seeing a revival in the island nation with more and more Coffee shops in Colombo sourcing locally rather than importing.

37. THEMED CAFES

Themed cafes are all the rage it appears, but Sri Lanka still has only a handful. Sri Lanka is a Cricket crazy nation and it makes sense that we have a 'Cricket Café' on Flower Road. Any Cricket enthusiast would be thrilled to see the walls plastered with Cricket memorabilia and signed bats, leather balls and Cricket t-shirts and the quirky menu with fun spins on names of famous cricketers. An absolute favourite at the Cricket Café is the Shepherd's Pie. Oh Yum!

Trivia- Sri Lanka won the Cricket World Cup in 1996 and the Twenty-Twenty (T20) World Cup in

2014. Interestingly, the national sport of Sri Lanka is beach Volleyball, not Cricket.

For Rugby fans there is a Rugby themed café intriguingly named as 'Blackout Restaurant & café' in Colombo 7. Whether this is because Rugby players mostly end up blacked out post match (as is the case with my hubby) or because Sri Lankans for some weird reason have an overwhelming love for the All Blacks Rugby team, is to be discovered.

Another recent themed café to pop up was 'Central Perk' for all the die-hard Friends fans in Colombo (myself included of course). However, though it shares the name of the actual Central Perk franchise it does not have all the Friends memorabilia and merchandise. Food is named after the characters and some of their quirky behavior such as "Joey doesn't share food!". The Orange couch is there for a Photo op and Monica's Purple door with the Mirror Frame is there as well. Other than that, it is yet another café to hang out with friends and chow down.

Eat Like a Local

38. A CUP OF JOE AND A GOOD BOOK IS ALL ONE NEEDS

For a book lover such as myself that is definitely true. 'Coffee and Pages' on Stratford Avenue is one such place that agrees and tries to cater to the 'niche' market of readers, in this day and age. But the best in my opinion is 'Chapters' in Colombo 4. It's the local equivalent of 'Borders Bookshop' on a much smaller scale. Though it may not have a Starbucks within the premises, what they do have is a cosy sofa and a yummy, delicious Hot Chocolate, where anyone can snuggle up and read a good book while sipping on a great Hot Chocolate.

39. SOUL HUNGERS FOR ART, TUMMY RUMBLES FOR FOOD...

For an art lover, there are several great galleries within Colombo that entices the soul. A favourite is 'Barefoot' Gallery in Colombo 4. The place is wonderful as it has a shop that sells handlooms reflecting the bright and beautiful colours of this exotic tropical island, a gallery in which to please the aesthetic sense and a garden café in which to relax and enjoy some well prepared food. A favourite is their milkshake, during a hot and humid day. 'Paradise Road Gallery' on Alfred House road is yet another wonderful place for the art lover and is located in the former offices of world-renowned Sri Lankan architect Geoffrey Bawa. The gallery runs through the section which houses the Café as well, aptly named 'The Gallery Café'. The food is great and the ambience brings 'paradise' into the city at a relatively higher price.

The National Art Gallery and Saskia Fernando Gallery are a few other places to visit but for the local yet undiscovered talent to truly be seen, just take a walk along Green Path during the daytime, as it is home to the local artists, displaying their beautiful work along the pavement.

Eat Like a Local

40. GRUB FEST

Every 3-4 months Green Path in Colombo puts together some amazing food festivals. It is a number of stalls of already established restaurants and home bakers, coming together to create a social event where foodies can walk along and enjoy various types of, mostly Sri Lankan, goodies.

'Eat Street CMB' is a favourite and has 'Achcharu' (pronounced 'Ah-ch-cha-ru') which has got to be the number 1 food item locals flock to when in need of a tangy, spicy snack with a kick! It is a combination of fruit such as Mango, Pineapple, Local Olives (known as 'Veralu'), Ambarella and sometimes Wood Apple in a mixture of salt and chili that will make your eyes water and nose drip, but that is all part of the 'Achcharu' experience. If you would rather not rub shoulders with locals patronizing the food festivals organized on Green Path and opt for an upscale food festival, the Hilton Colombo has launched Hawker Street at Graze Kitchen with food from Sri Lanka, India, Vietnam, China, Turkey and Japan.

41. CONFESSIONS OF A CHOCAHOLIC

When I want sunshine and smiles, all I need to do is to bite into a bar of Chocolate. Are there any other kindred spirits out there? Whether you are Chocaholic like me or not, Chocolate shops are not hard to come by in Colombo. 'Gerard Mendis Chocolatier' is just one name that pops to mind as a more upscale Chocolate haven in Colombo. But for those on a budget, fear not, Chocolate awaits you at more affordable places such as the 'Kandos Chocolate Shop' located at Thurstan Road and the 'Revello Specialty Chocolate' stall at Crescat Shopping Mall.

For Chocolate baked into a warm, gooey cookie, 'Brick Lane' is the place to go. If you are at Crescat Shopping Mall just rely on your nostrils to lead the way, as the aroma of cookies baking permeates the building from the Food Court located in the basement. 'Triple Chocolate', 'Nutella Burst' and 'Red Velvet' are some of my absolute favourites and I can never resist these cookies.

Eat Like a Local

Craving for Meringue slapped together with loads of Chocolate cream? Mrs. G's' Chocolate Meringue is the only one of its kind in Colombo, located at Carlwil Place. This is a home bakery and therefore needs pre booking and pick up and payment in cash. There are a plethora of Home Bakers who offer the usual Cupcakes, Brownies and Cookies and it is easy to find them through review sites if the preference is for some home baked goodies over mass produced items.

42. IS THERE EVEN SUCH A THING AS 'TOO MUCH SUGAR'?

I'm sure many health conscious people would answer with a vehement 'of course!', but I certainly am not one of them. Those who have a sweet tooth such as myself, are truly in sugar heaven when roaming in Colombo as there is no shortage of sweet treats for those who love to indulge in simple guilty pleasures.

'Hyve' in Colombo with décor resembling a beehive has sinfully chocolatey desserts, with a favourite being a jar of chocolate fudge! For moist, melt in your mouth, delectable cakes 'Sits' and 'The Cake Factory' are my personal favourites. Bonus Tip: The Perfect Chocolate cake at The Cake Factory is truly worthy of its name.

For gooey brownies chock full of choc chips I absolutely love 'Tea Avenue' brownies, which are warmed up prior to serving and simply ooze perfection. For perfect New York style cheesecake 'The Coffee Bean and Tea Leaf' serves up one of the best so far.

Ice cream in the heat of a tropical island is of course welcome, and a personal favourite is 'City Rest Fort' on Hospital Street, which serves up more than just the usual Chocolate & Vanilla options. Their Coconut ice cream is a taste of paradise isle. 'Il Gelato' and 'Baskin Robbins' are also available in Colombo.

43. LOVE AT FIRST BITE

For a Sri Lankan dessert experience, Buffalo Curd with Kitul (pronounced 'Key-Thul') Treacle or sometimes Jaggery for some crunch is a favourite among all in Sri Lanka. And what is not to love? Perfectly fermented Buffalo milk in clay pots is velvety and smooth with a molten Gold drizzle of treacle and some shards of crunchy yet soft and chewy Jaggery is enough for a mind boggling dessert experience. For the best curd the only name to remember is 'Hondahitha' (pronounced 'Ho-n-the-he-thuh) curd shop in Nugegoda. Although Waffles are not a local food item it is worth a mention here as this curd shop serves up some spectacular waffles that may or may not include some curd. It is hard to say.

Pol Pani Pancakes (Sweet treacle drenched coconut in crepes) is another Sri Lankan favourite. For a tasty version of this, 'Culinary Ceylon' on Hospital Street serves it.

44. ELEVATE YOUR SENSES

They say eating is an experience of all the senses. Sight, Touch, Smell, Sound and Taste. So it is only right that you experience your meal with all 5 senses in Colombo. But why restrict the senses to only the sight, smell, sound, feel and taste of the food being consumed, when a good view certainly makes any meal that much better?

To elevate the senses with elevated views of the city 'Celavi' at Kingsbury Hotel is a rooftop bar and lounge in which to witness history in the making with a bird's eye view of the Port City being built. 'Elevate' at Access towers offers a city view, as well as 'Botanik' which overlooks the twin towers, home to many businesses in the heart of the business district. Heading slightly out of Colombo to the suburbs to 'Sugar Beach' Mount Lavinia to catch a sunset, will not be a regret. It is great for a day out with family and they even allow pets.

For a poor man's experience of eating with a view, the Galle Face Green beckons with plenty of street vendors, the sound of the Indian Ocean and a spectacular view of the sunset right in the middle of Colombo.

45. MEET FOR MEAT

Love meat and can't live without it? Sri Lanka has it all, though it may not be easy to buy Veal and Duck etc. at supermarkets if the idea is to cook the meat by oneself. But for anyone else like myself, who only like to step into the kitchen when it's time to bake sweet treats, then there are plenty of places in Colombo to choose from when looking for perfectly cooked meat.

When anyone talks about meat what instantly comes to mind is a good steak and there are many options for a good steak in Colombo. A personal favourite is 'Rare' at Park Street, which serves up some local flavours along with well-established flavour combinations, paving the way for an amazing food experience. This is also a good location for a date night as mentioned earlier. 'The Bavarian' in Colombo and 'The Grill' at the Kingsbury Hotel are other noteworthy places for an amazing steak.

For BBQ cravings 'M'eat us Grill' on Flower Road is known for their amazing spare ribs. It is also BYOB, corkage free. It's a really good place to chow down and wind down with some good wine and some good company.

46. GO VEG

Vegetarians and Vegans may not have many options in Colombo apart from the Indian restaurants, but one place to cater to this niche but growing crowd is 'Milk and Honey' down Horton Place. Although they have introduced some meat items to their menu for the carnivorous majority, they are still a Vegan and Vegetarian friendly place.

For Indian vegetarian food there are many options with 'Shanmugas' in Colombo 6 being a favourite. Most restaurants will have a few Vegetarian options on their menus but Vegans may not find it easy to find an extensive menu to choose from.

Eat Like a Local

47. AFTER PARTY FOOD

From bar hopping to club hopping, either way you end up on the streets in the wee hours of the morning in search of some grub. 'Pilawoos' is the go to place for all locals for some tasty Sri Lankan food. Everyone's favourite Cheese Koththu is something to try. Pilawoos is located in almost every town and sometimes is known as 'Hotel de Pilawoos' or 'Grand Pilawoos'.

'Burger's King' in Slave Island is not the franchise 'Burger King'. What it is, is a street vendor who started with a tiny cart of food along the pavement and now has a restaurant in the same location, serving up the best Shawarma in town.

Most hotels cater to the party-goers with early morning breakfast, when it doesn't seem like a good idea to be walking the streets in the wee hours of the morning in a foreign land.

48. GOOD MARKET, GOOD PRODUCE, GOOD TIMES

Anyone who has ever watched an episode of 'My Sri Lanka with Peter Kuruvita' will be eager to cook a Sri Lankan meal while in the island. So where do you go to get good produce? While all supermarkets have what you need from fresh vegetables grown in chilly Nuwaraeilya, to fresh seafood caught that very day by our fishermen, for some unbeatable prices and good produce Colpetty market is a great place. Some haggling skills are required and getting there early is recommended, as the produce tends to sell out fast. For the freshest of fresh seafood, 'Sirilak' on the outskirts of Colombo is another place to visit early as possible to get the required quantity of fresh seafood.

Good Market available daily at 'Lakpahana' on Reid Avenue or Battaramulla (suburb) has a heavy screening process and is the best place for organic produce. For a better experience of the Good Market, there is a Saturday event which houses many stalls and has better prices, located at the Race Course Mall. It also gives the opportunity to savour some of the amazing home cooked treats, which are sold at

Eat Like a Local

these stalls on Saturdays. 'Cheese Hoppers' in the morning are a great way to start the day while getting the grocery shopping done.

For Sri Lankan spices, Ma's or Koluu's available at all leading supermarkets, are the better brands. The latter is better known for various curry mixes, making it easy to get the authentic Sri Lankan taste in curry. Bonus Tip- Make 'Pol Roti' (Coconut flat bread) as it is not difficult to make and can be enjoyed hot off the stove with just some drippy, melted butter if unable to make a curry or sambol to go with it.

49. GETTING FRUITY

Tangy Passion Fruit, Juicy Mango, Pungent Durian, Funky Woodapple, Spiky Rambutan, Prickly Pineapple, Perfect Avocado, Delicious Papaya, Sweet Soursop, Anti-oxidizing Pomegranate, Velvety Mangosteen… the list is endless and lets not forget the many varieties of Bananas available in Sri Lanka.

Although it may not be a favourite place to frequent, from time to time I feel the urge to jump into the chaotic world of the Pettah Market to find the best fruit. It is recommended to wear covered shoes when visiting the Pettah Market as it is not the cleanest of locations in Colombo.

For those who just cannot put up with the chaos of the market and would rather just get some good fruit at a more convenient location, 'Fresheez' by CIC has good produce and they also make fresh juices. 'Roots' is yet another option for refreshing juice variations best suited for Colombo's heat and humidity.

Fruit Salad is a firm favourite with every local as it makes them feel happy to indulge in something 'healthy' or as healthy as it can be with sugar mixed in or a huge dollop of Vanilla ice cream over the Fruit Salad. The perfect roadside place for the perfect fruit salad is at Bristol Street, right opposite the Commercial Bank. It doesn't get any better than standing along the road, amidst traffic and enjoying a huge bowl full of freshly prepared fruit salad.

Eat Like a Local

50. TEA-SPIRATIONS

Sri Lanka is a Tea Country, so naturally we are Tea inspired and infuse Tea into our food. Although it is not widely popular among the majority of the locals yet, tea infusion is making it self known to the Sri Lankan palate and no one does it better than the Tea expert, Dilmah. 'The t-lounge by Dilmah' is a great option for any Tea lover with Tea inspired burgers, pizza subs, ice cream and desserts. They have fun Tea Pairing options to choose from as well. For those looking for gifts to take back for family and friends, 'The t-lounge by Dilmah' has some great varieties and flavours can be mixed and matched as well.

For a true Ceylon Cinnamon with Ceylon Tea experience, Dilmah has a multitude of flavours that include Ceylon Cinnamon.

Heladiv Tea Club at Dutch Hospital is also a good place for Tea Lovers with yummy food and some pretty good desserts. An absolute favourite is their take on an Iced Tea Soda.

Eat Like a Local

BONUS TIPS

One doesn't truly experience Sri Lanka by spending their time only in Colombo. The below bonus tips are on some of my favourite places in the island, for the traveler who is looking to venture out and experience the country as a whole.

1. SUN, SAND & SURF

When in an island nation the beach is never too far away. We are spoilt for choice with locations to choose from when in need of some fun in the sun. Below is a guide to some of my favourite places when in need of some sea breeze, tangled hair and sand in between my toes.

Down South-
Galle fort and the Dutch Hospital shopping precinct in Galle awaits the traveller searching for a bit of history and some amazing food. Dondra Head is the southern most point of the teardrop shaped island and worth a visit. The Literary Festival is hosted in Galle every year for the book worms such as myself. For

those who are more into nature than books, Whale Watching in Mirissa is great and sometimes the Whale watchers are lucky enough to see some playful Dolphins as well. For the beach bums the clearest Blue waters can be found in Unawatuna and Weligama is excellent for catching that perfect wave. For those who like to party all the time, Hikkaduwa is known for the best beach parties.

North & East Coast-
A previously war ravaged area that was inaccessible for nearly 3 decades, is now a vibrant tourist destination beckoning tourist and locals alike, as majority of locals were unable to visit these parts of the island during the civil war. An absolute favourite is Trincomalee in the North East with its Marble Beach and Green Bay in pristine condition. It is also the perfect place to rise early and watch that sunrise. Arugambay is known as the surfer's paradise. Jaffna boasts flavours of its own and is home to the amazing Karthokolomban Mango, which is the most amazing and juiciest mango within the shores of Sri Lanka. Jaffna is also home to Point Pedro, which is the northern most point of Sri Lanka.

Eat Like a Local

West Coast-
For a quick drive and some amazing seafood and roadside bistros, Negombo is excellent. An absolute favourite is 'Prego' which serves up some delectable Italian dishes. They also have an extensive Wine list and it is heavenly to have a nice chilled glass of White Wine in the heat of Negombo. The best lagoon Crab can be found in many restaurants in Negombo.

2. KINGDOM PAST

Kandy- though it is not the last Kingdom of old Sri Lanka it is the place that is most associated with kings of a bygone era. It is also home to the Temple of the Tooth Relic. Kandy town is worth a visit on foot as there is a beautiful walk around the lake that simply beckons foreigners and locals alike. Also, it makes sense to walk in Kandy rather than drive as the town is terribly congested. 'Mlesna Tea Center' is the ideal place to get some rest after walking around Kandy town, while enjoying a perfect cuppa and some light snacks.

3. CENTRAL HIGHLANDS

Little England in Sri Lanka, better known as Nuwaraeliya is a place I love and have visited at least once a year since I was a kid. It is the perfect place to escape to when in desperate need to get away from the extreme heat as temperatures average between 51-68 Fahrenheit (in no means frigid, but pleasantly cool). Heritance Tea Factory is an amazing place for an incredible dining experience, while the Grand Hotel Nuwaraeliya takes you back to the time when the British colonized the island as it is steeped in history. It is also an excellent place for High Tea. A visit to the strawberry farm where you can also eat fresh strawberries and cream is an excellent way to spend a morning. New Zealand farm and Ambewela farm are adjoining each other and is an educational experience and as a bonus offers some excellent views along with the chance to pet some incredibly cute farm animals. Lake Gregory is a chilled out place for a cool walk or even a chilly picnic. While located in Nuwaraeliya, make some day trips out to Diyatalawa, Bandarawela and Ella and stop along the way to see the amazing waterfalls that Sri Lanka has been blessed with. A personal favourite was the St.

Clair's Waterfall in Hatton, which at times has been known as the Bridal Veil for its sheer, mesmerizing beauty. Now, however due to the water being diverted to a nearby hydro power station, it is no longer considered the most beautiful waterfall in Sri Lanka, but we still do have plenty more.

4. DRY ZONE

An area steeped in history, with remains / ruins of the works of many past kings, still standing proudly to show off the splendor and culture of Sri Lanka. A visit to Sri Lanka is incomplete without taking in the sites of Anuradhapura and Polonnaruwa. The heat is extreme and the air is dry. Be sure to stay hydrated and there are plenty of restaurants to get some good food.

5. NATIVE LANKANS IN DAMBANA

Veddhas (pronounced 'Vah-D-Dah') meaning 'the people of the forest' are considered to be the aborigines of Sri Lanka and many consider them to the be the first inhabitants of the island prior to the arrival of King Vijaya in the island. The Veddha minority in Sri Lanka is soon to be extinct and the language is dying out as only Veddhas who live in tribes in certain areas of the country such as Dambana still speak it. The rest of the citizens speak Sinhala. Veddha Village tours in Dambana are organized for the traveler, eager to see how the early man lived in the island.

WHY VISIT?

1. Culture

Sri Lanka is indeed a cultural melting pot with many different influences on food, architecture, religion and lifestyle. It may come as a surprise to many, as Sri Lanka is a developing country, that the literacy levels are high in Sri Lanka and males and females share equal status in education and power. The first female prime minister of the world was in Sri Lanka (Sirimavo Bandaranaike).

Take a trip into history and discover about the kings of Sri Lanka to know about their quirky habits (such as King Kassapa of Sigiriya), to get an idea of the clothing of Sri Lanka back in the day, and how Sri Lanka gained independence. Now, westernized to a great extent, all locals wear modern attire while some continue to wear Saree which is mainly the Indian Saree, however Sri Lanka has a Saree that is unique to Sri Lanka, known as the Kandyan Saree. It may look similar to the Indian Saree to the un-trained eye but there are subtle differences.

The Sinhala language is mainly from Pali and Sanskrit and there are some similarities in Hindi and Sinhala languages. All road signs will be in all three languages used in Sri Lanka (i.e. English, Sinhala and Tamil) for the ease of all the citizens within the country.

2. Beauty

The island nation is indeed beautiful with its Golden sands and clear Blue waters, lush greenery and tea plantations covered in a veil of early morning mist, some incredible architecture dating back to the 16th Century and even the chaotic muddle of streets in Colombo is beautiful in its own way.

Blessed with natural beauty, the locals are yet to understand the best way to keep the beauty in tact by maintaining clean spaces and taking required care with waste, however this is changing with the 30 something's taking the lead in developing the nation and being open to new ideas.

Eat Like a Local

3. People

The people of any country are what make the land so inviting. Sri Lankan people are hospitable and will welcome anyone with toothy smiles from the time they arrive till the time they leave. They are happy to serve and will be at the constant beck and call of tourists.

> Sri Lanka is a poor nation economically, but we make up for it with our ready smiles and open arms, inviting you in to sit down and have a cup of Tea with us and to taste our amazing food. Take the memory of warmth and happiness back with you and let the people of Sri Lanka, living around the world, remind you that paradise really does exist in this world.

OTHER RESOURCES:

www.yamu.lk
www.pulse.lk
www.exploresrilanka.lk
www.tripadvisor.com

READ OTHER BOOKS BY CZYK PUBLISHING

Greater Than a Tourist- St. Croix US Birgin Islands USA: 50 Travel Tips from a Local by Tracy Birdsall

Greater Than a Tourist- Toulouse France: 50 Travel Tips from a Local by Alix Barnaud

Children's Book: *Charlie the Cavalier Travels the World* by Lisa Rusczyk

Eat Like a Local

Follow *Eat Like a Local* on Amazon.

Printed in Great Britain
by Amazon